●

1 · 9 · 9 · 9

CIP - kataložni zapis o publikaciji
Narodna in univerzitetna knjižnica, Ljubljana

82(497)-194

KNOTS : anthology of Southeastern European haiku / edited by
Dimitar Anakiev & Jim Kacian. - Tolmin : Prijatelj, 1999

ISBN 961-90715-0-6
1. Anakiev, Dimitar 2. Kacian, Jim
99124992

THE ANTHOLOGY OF SOUTHEASTERN EUROPEAN HAIKU POETRY

edited by
Dimitar Anakiev
&
Jim Kacian

Dimitar Anakiev

FROM MOVEMENT TO LITERATURE

Southeastern Europe, a mixture of many nations, religions, cultures and languages, has long been considered a cradle of European culture. In a geographic and cultural sense the Balkan peninsula represents a bridge between Europe and Asia, between West and East. This makes the Balkans (1) a perfect locale for participation in the expansion of the haiku here in the last days of the twentieth century.

Haiku came to the Balkans as early as 1878, though seriously and with a fuller comprehension of what the form was and could be only since 1927 (2), and has become the most popular literary form here over its next seven decades of development (3). More than 2000 people are writing haiku here — some simply amateurs and lovers of poetry, some professional writers and poets (4). It is not an exaggeration to say that Southeastern Europe is one of the new homelands of haiku poetry (5).

The book in front of you is the very first attempt to survey haiku in this region from its introduction into the area to the present. It tries to evaluate and place Balkan haiku in the context of the haiku literature of the West, and more generally of the world (6). In no other literary form (or, it may be said, in no other art form) does the art of the Balkans intertwine with the art of the World to so great an extent, or play, as it does, such a vanguard role. The editors of this volume were first and foremost interested in discovering and evaluating the authentic haiku art of the Balkans. All literary periods of haiku development in Southeast Europe were considered (7). However, an especial emphasis was place upon the present, it being most relevant and representative to us today. Special interest was paid to the recognition and understanding of the relationship between haiku movement, based mainly on haiku ideology, and authentic haiku art, which is more given to non—ideological artistic values.

When selecting haiku for this anthology, the primary consideration was given simply to the quality of individual poems. The most important element in determining quality was the *haiku moment* — its depth and purity.

Other elements considered included precision of imagery and delineation; unity of form and content; juxtaposition of and resonance between images; visual and aural polish. At the same time the formal framework of the traditional Japanese haiku (5-7-5 syllables) has proven for the most part superfluous for the authors in expressing their moments. This volume, then, will represent to some degree a removal from some theories of Japanese haiku. In addition, poems which are reminiscent of or based upon classical Japanese models have not been considered. Additionally, poems which rely upon metaphor or personification for their affect have not been considered. These are departures from previous editing policies in many haiku publications in our region.

After much consideration, we have chosen to include *war* as a general topic in this collection, but its action is not unlike that of kigo. Great political instability in the region (known worldwide as the "powderkeg") has forced our poets to consider that war has become almost a kind of a "seasonal" phenomenon which devastes Southeastern Europe on a regular basis, like a tornado, say, unexpected and yet predictable. This last decade of the century has been replete with such disaster. Among the many thousands of haiku which covered these events, it was decided to include only those which possessed a strong sense of the haiku moment, and which opened beyond the experience of war itself. Poems whose primary functions were similar to "protests", "comments", "astonishments", ultimtely prove inadequate as artistic statement, and have not found a place in this volume.

In the end, it was our hope to bring a new orientation to the editorial sensibility in Southeastern Europe, one which would depend neither on the cult of haiku nor upon the sanctifying of individual poets. The ultimate standard for haiku must be the poem itself, and the sensibility which we value in it must be our own, in our own time, in our own place. We believe this volume exhibits such values, across the artificial boundaries of countries and cultures, in a shared sensibility which unites poets beyond the ideologies imposed by states and ideas.

Knots surveys haiku from eleven countries (8), written in ten languages and many different syllabaries. The greater part of this collection originates from countries where haiku life is well organized (9). In some countries, however, where there is no haiku organization or apparatus, haiku is pursued simply by individuals (10). It has taken more than one year to complete this project, to collect the thousands of haiku worthy of consideration, and then to select from these the best and most representative of Balkan haiku. Such an extensive project could not be successfully completed without the cooperation of a great number of people. I would like to thank especially the poets who have shared their work: without them and their special gifts, there would be no Balkan haiku aesthetic, no Balkan haiku voice. Also, many editors from different countries and their translators contributed greatly to the production of this volume, including (in alphabetic order) Marijan Čekolj, President of the Croatian Haiku Society and Editor of the *Vrabac* haiku magazine, Samobor, Croatia;

Ion Codrescu, Editor of *Albatross* haiku magazine, Costanta, Romania; Milijan Despotović, Editor of the *Paun* haiku magazine, Požega, Yugoslavia; Zoran Doderović, Editor of *Haiku Moment* magazine, Novi Sad, Yugoslavia; Zoran Raonić, Editor of the *Anthology of Montenegro Haiku*, Pljevlja, Yugoslavia; Primož Repar, Editor of *Apokalipsa* magazine, Ljubljana, Slovenia; Dragan J. Ristić, Editor of the *Haiku Novine*, Niš, Yugoslavia; Nebojša Simin, Editor of the *Haiku Pismo*, Novi Sad, Yugoslavia; Dimitar Stefanov, Editor of Haiku Column in the *Literaturen Forum*, Sofia, Bulgaria; Bogdanka Stojanovski, Editor of the *Leaflet*, Novi Sad, Yugoslavia; Florin Vasiliu, President of the Romanian Haiku Society and Editor of the *Haiku* magazine, Bucharest; Vid Vukasović, Editor of the *Rainbow Petal*, e-magazine, Belgrade, Yugoslavia; Savina Zoe, Editor of the *World Haiku Anthology*, Pallini-Attikis, Greece. I'd like to express my personal gratitude to many others: Vladimir Devidé and Tom Noyes, old haiku friends, for useful suggestions and support; Alain Kervern for the text about this book; my old friends Mateja Špacapan and Igor Drnovšek from Tolmin for their translations from French into English; Alma and Zvonka for their support...

Finally, my immense gratitude goes to my fellow editors of Knots for their unselfish work: Slavoljub Stanković, with whom I have collaborated on haiku projects for seven years; and Jim Kacian, whose help and support was crucial for the birth of this book.

The readers will be able to find more details about the authors, their books, bibliography of haiku in the Balkans, history and development of haiku movement of this region, all about haiku clubs, associations and haiku publications in a book entitled Guide to Southeastern European Haiku, by the same authors, due out next year (2000) and to be published by Prijatelj Haiku Press.

(1) "Balkan" is a Turkish word meaning "Mountain". Most of the countries of Southeast Europe occupy the Balkan peninsula, which is bounded by the rivers Danube, Sava and Soča, except Romania. But history and culture links Romania and the Balkans (Romania took part in the Balkan war, in 1913, for example). Other hand, the Balkans are the heart of Southeast Europe and we may use the terms "Southeast Europe" and "the Balkans" as synonyms.
(2) Bogdan Patriceicu Hasdeu translated for the first time Japanese poetry into Romanian in 1878, but a more influential and accurate translation into Serbian was *Poezija starog Japana*, by Miloš Crnjanski, Matica srpska, Novi Sad, 1927; in Bulgarian in 1943 *Poezia na Yamato* translated by Nikola Dzerov; in Croatian *Mala antologija japanskog haikua* by Dubravko Ivančan, Republika, Zagreb, 1966, in Slovenian *Mala antologija japonske lirike* by Mart Ogen, Ljubljana, 1974. The first poet who published his own haiku in a volume was Romanian Al. T. Stamatiad: *Peisagii Sentimentale*, Adevarul press, 1936, followed by *Leptirova krila* by Dubravko Ivančan in 1964.

12

(3) The crucial moment for the development and understanding of haiku in former Yugoslavia was *Japanska haiku poezija...* by Vladimir Devidé, Zagreb 1970, and then the appearance of the first European haiku magazines *Haiku* (1978-1981) in Varaždin, and *Paun* (1988) in Požega, while in Romania a crucial text was *Interferente lirice-Constalatia Haiku* by Florin Vasiliu and Brandusa Steiciuc, Buchurest, 1989. The first Romanian haiku magazine Haiku, edited by Florin Vasiliu, premiered in 1990. The first Haiku Festival & Contest in former Yugoslavia started in Odžaci in 1987, organized by Vojislav Milenković. The first international haiku meeting The Constanta International Haiku Festival organized by Ion Codrescu in Constanca, Romania, in June 1992.

(4) Some of the outstanding national poets who also wrote haiku include: Milan Dekleva from Slovenia, Luko Paljetak from Croatia, Desanka Maksimović and Dobrica Erić from Serbia, Nichita Stanescu from Romania, Dimitar Stefanov from Bulgaria and George Seferis from Greece.

(5) At the moment there are 12 haiku associations and 17 haiku publications in Southeastern Europe.

(6) Amongst many acknowledgements from different competitions in all parts of the World we should mention some principal awards: Darko Plažanin, JAL Grand Prix 1990; Dimitar Anakiev, MDN Second Prize in 1993; Ion Codrescu, HSA Grand Prize 1996; Dan Doman, MDN First Prize 1997; Busioc E. Valentin, MDN Second Prize 1997; Vid Vukasović, MDN First Prize 1998.

(7) In former Yugoslavia (in Serbian and Croatian languages) haiku went through the following stages:
  a. Pioneer Period /non-systematic development 1927- 1970/
  b. Period of the Haiku Movement /1970-1990/
  c. Period of the Haiku Literature /from 1990/

(7) Albania, Bosnia & Hercegovina, Bulgaria, Croatia, Cyprus, Greece, FYR Macedonia, Romania, Slovenia, Turkey, Yugoslavia.

(9) Haiku societies in Southeastern Europe were founded in the following order: The Romanian Haiku Society founded in 1991 by Florin Vasiliu; The Croatian Haiku Association, founded by Marijan Čekolj in 1992, Haiku Club "Masaoka Shiki" Niš, Yugoslavia, founded by Dimitar Anakiev in 1993.

(10) Dimitar Stefanov is editing a monthly Haiku Column in Literaturen Forum, a major literary paper in Bulgaria, since 1998.

Jim Kacian

TAPPING THE COMMON WELL

What is it about haiku that cannot be defeated?

It has no particular academic standing. It has no wealthy benefactor. It has no patron saint. It does not appear, at least in a form that serious practitioners would recognize, in the mainstream media. Though many people have heard of the word, few can offer even a single example, and those who can usually quote a poem in translation that is over three hundred years old. Even the most serious of scholars can hardly agree upon a definition of the term. When it is taught in schools, it is nearly always taught incorrectly, with the wrong emphases. And yet despite all these impediments, haiku is more a part of international literature and culture today than ever before. How can this be?

The reason, I believe, is simple and important. Haiku, in its many manifestations, offers something to people that simply they must have: a way to speak of the things they value in their lives, large and small, in ways that are communicable to others. Other art forms often require considerable grounding in theories and techniques, but haiku are simple and clean. This is not to say they are easy to create: they are as easy as any clean and simple truth, which is to say, difficult in the extreme. But they offer the possibility of such communication which is out of reach for most through the medium of painting, for example, or music. It is an available art, and one's success in it seems almost assured through repeated exposure and practice.

This, then, is the epistemological grounding of haiku, but there is an aesthetic one as well. There can be no gainsaying the poet's moment of insight, truth, clarity, oneness with the world. But how well he or she communicates it is a matter that affects us all. If the goal of the poet is to help the reader recreate the moment for himself, then the skill with which the poem is constructed and displayed becomes central to its availability to the reader. Haiku thus becomes a literary art, not merely a religious or philosophical one, and as such may be judged in terms of literary values. It takes a very great artist to be deep and simple at the same time, and not leave her thumbprint all over the poem. That is why it is adjudged a great feat to create a perfect haiku—not just because one has seen the truth, but because one has communicated it.

Haiku is elemental, like water. Though it has come to us from Japan, it is no more Japanese than water. Nor is it English, the language of this volume, or Slovenian or Bantu. Like water, it is universal, instantly recognized for what it is anywhere. Like water, it arises from a deep place which underlies all our common ground, unaware of the temporary boundaries that men may place on the surface above it. It may emerge in a great many places and in different forms. It may have a slightly different taste in one region, may stagnate in another, may be fresh or salty, thin as vapor or hard as ice, but it is still recognizably itself. This is because it does not trade in the relative truths of nationalities or religions, but rather in the universal truths between people. This does not mean it will appear the same to all people, to a rain-forest dwellers and a desert bedouin: there are always points of view. But haiku express values beyond regional and economic differences, revealing the truth of things as they are, which is at the core of how we feel most deeply as people. Haiku finds that which is not superfluous in the hearts of men, and expresses the values found there, as deep as that may go.

Haiku, then, offer, moment to moment, the truths of the lives of the poets who fashion them. War, beauty, nature, peace, ugliness, light and shadow—wherever insight is encountered, there the poet finds sustenance. These truths, when well expressed, are communicable to others without reference to political or religious affiliation, far beyond polemic or idealogy. For this is where truth resides, and however much it might have been misused for polemical purposes in the past, it has no place here, in the hearts of those who would seek and share the insight of such moments. This is what is indestructible in haiku, what has made it grow from one nation's cultural export to a world's form of choice to reveal the truth and beauty of the deep moments, the connected moments, of our lives.

●

Abăluță Konstantin, ROMANIA

(1)
trees in the mist—
climbing my arm
an ant

Adjanski Pavle, YUGOSLAVIA

●

(2)   wheat waves waves waves to the horizon

Alexe Gabriele, ROMANIA

●

(3)
climbing the mountain—
edelweiss fills
the blue sky

Anakiev Alma, SLOVENIA

(4)

virgin forest—
on the beech root, shadows
of many trees

Anakiev Dimitar, SLOVENIA

●

(5)
new year's eve—
the window sill gathers
dead flies

Anakiev Dimitar, SLOVENIA

(6)
hot chestnuts—
the first snow melts
upon them

Anakiev Dimitar, SLOVENIA

●

(7)
spring evening—
the wheel of a troop carrier
crushes a lizard

Bambić Maša, CROATIA

(8)
patters and drums
on the turtle's carapace
spring rain

Bebek Robert, CROATIA

(9)
meeting each other
then disappearing—
footprints in snow

Bebek Robert, CROATIA

my best friend died—
some tiny grains of dust
on our chess-board

Bebek Robert, CROATIA

(11)

wearing their homes
only in their eyes—
the refugees

Banea Ştefan, ROMANIA

(12)

moonlit lake—
the muzzle of a deer
touches the water

Bilankov Smiljka, CROATIA

a sunbeam
through bare branches—
new buds

Bizjak Zvonka, SLOVENIA

(14)
waving grass—
the words of my friend
i remember

Boban Nediljko, CROATIA

(15)
wide field—
everywhere the old man digs
sun finds the hoe

Boban Nedilјko, CROATIA

●

(16)   from the snail's shell
droplets
of mountain rain

Božin Mirjana, YUGOSLAVIA

(17)
autumn night—
a ladder leans against
the full moon

Bratić Ilija, YUGOSLAVIA

(18)
first screams
from the tiny magpie—
spring sun

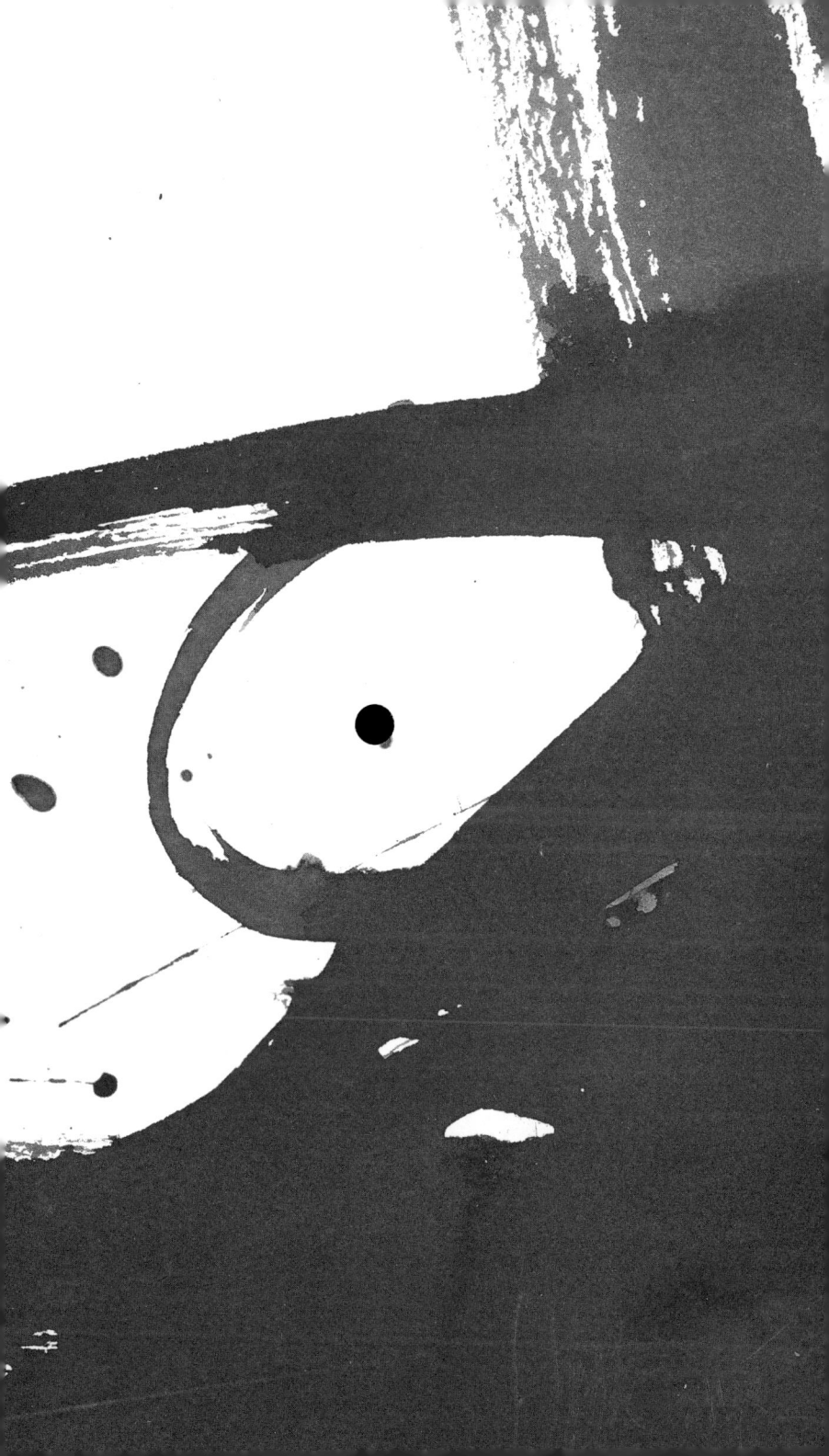

Brcanović Valentina, YUGOSLAVIA

●

(19)
the smell of quince—
on the window pane
snowflakes are melting

Brnović Veselin, YUGOSLAVIA

(20)
waft of lilac—
spring morning blows
into my room

Bubanja Vojislav, YUGOSLAVIA

(21)
park bench—
a maple leaf clings
to wet paint

Bukva Borivoj, CROATIA

along the deserted coast
the waves are quieting down—
the end of the day

Busioc E. Valentin, ROMANIA

(23)
frosty winter—
the smooth curve
of the axe handle

Busioc E. Valentin, ROMANIA

(24)
stones...
among them
the snake's breath

Busioc E. Valentin, ROMANIA

(25)
drinking water from my palm—
sand settles
in the life line

Bušić Franko, CROATIA

winter darkness...
there, just for the moment
scent of the ocean

Čekolj Marijan, CROATIA

(27)
first autumn rain—
the murmur from a waterfall
grows loud

Čekolj Marijan, CROATIA

●

(28) where the sky
touches the earth
thunder

Čekolj Marijan, CROATIA

(29)
terminal—
passing in waves
the murmur of voices

Čevanić Majska, CROATIA

(30)
the fish-market—
the slack mouth of a carp
clings to the grass

Ćirović - Ljutički Milenko, YUGOSLAVIA

●

(31)
waterfall—
snowdrops nearby
bob their heads

Codrescu Ion, ROMANIA

(32)
redecorated house—
under the eaves a sparrow
begins its nest

Codrescu Ion, ROMANIA

(33)
end of the party—
first dry leaves
come into the verandah

Codrescu Ion, ROMANIA

●

(34)
after the concert
clearing the car of snow
not a world is said

Čopa Miroslav, YUGOSLAVIA

(35)
winter morning—
the candle in the old photo
is still burning

Čopa Miroslav, YUGOSLAVIA

(36)
full moon—
shadows and people
travel by train

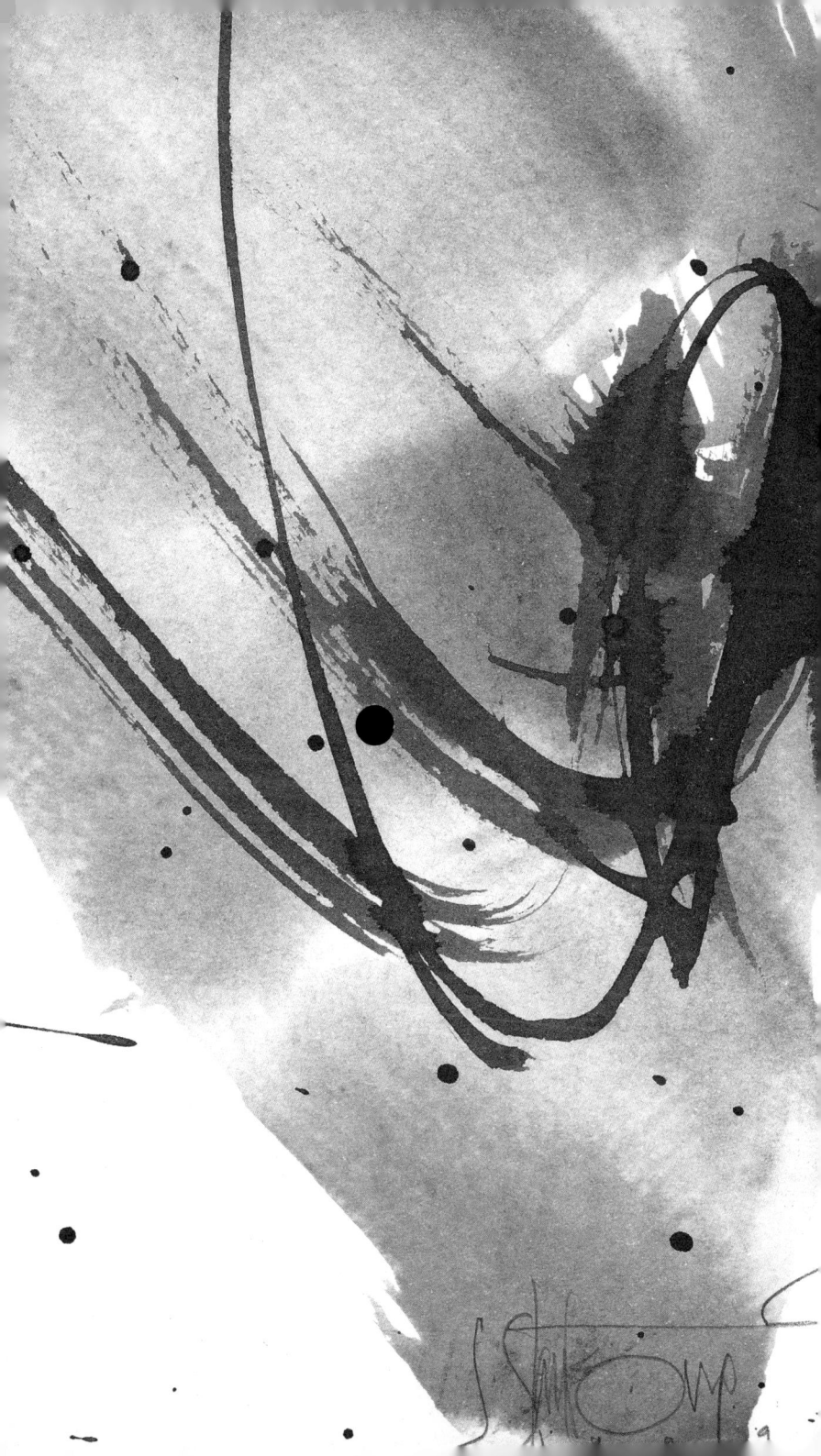

THE ANTHOLOGY OF SOUTHEASTERN EUROPEAN HAIKU POETRY · THE ANTHOLOGY OF SOUTHEASTERN EUROPEAN HAIKU POETRY · THE ANTHOLOGY OF SOUTHEASTERN EURO

Ciubotariu Manta Elena, ROMANIA

(37)

trike ride—
the child races
his shadow

Crnomarković Ileana, CROATIA

●

(38)
rooster's crow—
from the dark sea darker
voices of fisherman

Cvetanović Vidoje, YUGOSLAVIA

(39)
meadow—
after gleaning the hay,
the remaining smell

Cvetković Predrag, YUGOSLAVIA

(40)
over the wet forest
wind is blowing around
a patch of fog

Cvetković Predrag, YUGOSLAVIA

(41)
snowy fields—
it's getting dark first
among bare willows

Dacić Rade, YUGOSLAVIA

(42)
a single stone
protrudes from the grass—
our former home

Dejanović Goran, YUGOSLAVIA

●

(43)
the bell's jingling
at the entrance to the village—
twilight

Denjo Mirsad, B & H

(44)
sparrow and magpie—
a sip each
from the same puddle

Devidé Vladimir, CROATIA

(45)
in each eye
of the child—two eyes
of a puppy

Devidé Vladimir, CROATIA

(46)
a small pool of blood—
killed in the air-raid: a little girl
and her huge blond doll

Devidé Vladimir, CROATIA

(47)
traveling by car—
the setting sun is rolling
down the pine forest

Dimić Moma, YUGOSLAVIA

●

(48) even the urine stream
belongs to my shadow—
moonlit night

Djurbabić Svetomir, YUGOSLAVIA

●

(49)
vineyard—
the metal rasp of scissors
dissects the silence

Djuričić Ljiljana, YUGOSLAVIA

sudden shower—
i share the store eaves
with a stranger

Djurišić Dušan, YUGOSLAVIA

●

(51)
dewy grass:
the silvery fillet
of a snail

Djurišić Dušan, YUGOSLAVIA

(52)
bursting
out of the ripe rye:
red poppies

Doderović Zoran, YUGOSLAVIA

(53)
scent of hyacinth
fills the empty room—
mother's birthday

Doderović Zoran, YUGOSLAVIA

(54)
a cup of tea
shaking in the old woman's hand
summer clouds

Doderović Zoran, YUGOSLAVIA

●

(55)   detonations—
the X of tape on the pane
divides the sky

Doman Dan, ROMANIA

●

(56)
leafless trees—
sun sets
amidst the crows

Doman Dan, ROMANIA

(57)
house on the hill—
out of a chimney scatters
the Milky Way

Dumitresku Emilia, ROMANIA

(58)   full flower:
copious bindweed
cover the brambles

Dumitru Radu, ROMANIA

glassy lake—
the oar gathers
sun and willows

Duţu Olga, ROMANIA

(60)
among weeds and shells
the seahorse waiting
for a wave

Faraon Eugenia, ROMANIA

(61)
early morning—
the first shine on the fence
a snail's trail

Funda Željko, CROATIA

(62)
a leaf
patching a hole
in my shoe

Gagić Smiljka, CROATIA

(63)
remains of a ship—
down the coast
a boy rinses shells

Gašpar Dragica, YUGOSLAVIA

(64)
gleaned field—
sweet-smelling silence
and voices of quail

Gečić Anica, CROATIA

●

(65)
cease-fire:
the wedding goes off
to the sound of cannon

Hamazin Ana, CROATIA

●

(66)　the sun setting
down the cracked cliff into
the sound of the sea

Hohnjec Josip, YUGOSLAVIA

●

(67) a flicker of light
in a well illuminates
the yellow leaves

Hudnik Marko, SLOVENIA

(68)
rain stopped—
the last train enters
the wood flowers' smell

Iacob P. Ion, ROMANIA

●

(69) autumn storm—
the postman
shivers

Ifrim Clilea, ROMANIA

(70)
a thread of sand
in the empty piggy-bank—
summer is gone

Ilijevska - Jovanovska Pandora, MACEDONIA

(71)
after the rain—
a snail glowing
in the grass

Ioannou Costas, GREECE

(72)
the doctor's diagnosis
of my dizziness:
"spring fever"

Isaic Cătălin, ROM

(73)
from time to time
the cigarette smoke blurs
grandpa's face

Ivančan Dubravko, CROATIA

(74)
early thaw—
gravel slides
beneath the tires

Ivančan Dubravko, CROATIA

(75)
dim night—
snow falls before
the street lamp

Ivančan Dubravko, CROATIA

(76)
green meadow—
slant necks of the geese
through the grass

Jegdić Branka, YUGOSLAVIA

(77)
hide' n' seek—
flowers in her hair
hop at each step

Jembrih Ivica, CROATIA

(78)
through the window
sunbeams refract
in the infusion bottle

Joksimović Zorica, YUGOSLAVIA

●

(79)
barely legible
on the faded nightgown:
je t' aime

Jovanović Bojan, YUGOSLAVIA

●

(80)
an old forest—
fine particles of its ruins
are carried away by ants

Kalač Hamdija, YUGOSLAVIA

(81)
deserted room—
in a dark corner tomcat
twists the moonlight

Kovačević Ivan, CROATIA

(82)
jumping—
a boy
and grasshopper

Kovačević Ivan, CROATIA

(83)
mutual understanding:
a tramp and scarecrow
exchange hats

Krizmanić Franjo, B & H

(84)
grandpa's forge fire—
cherries redden
in the glow

Mančić Olga - Lodika, YUGOSLAVIA

●

(85)
a pathway—
the gentle look of a priest
in silence

Manić - Forski Dragoslav, YUGOSLAVIA

●

(86)
eyes of an icon
from the ruined church
watching the sky

Maretić Tomislav, CROATIA

(87)
a child shakes
the first snow from the swing—
quiet morning

Maretić Tomislav, CROATIA

(88)
the guests are coming—
are the petals to be swept
away from the path ?

Maretić Tomislav, CROATIA

(89)
burn site—
on the spared fence
morning glories

Marijanović Dubravko, CROATIA

(90)
hot noon—
dustman's car
zigzagging

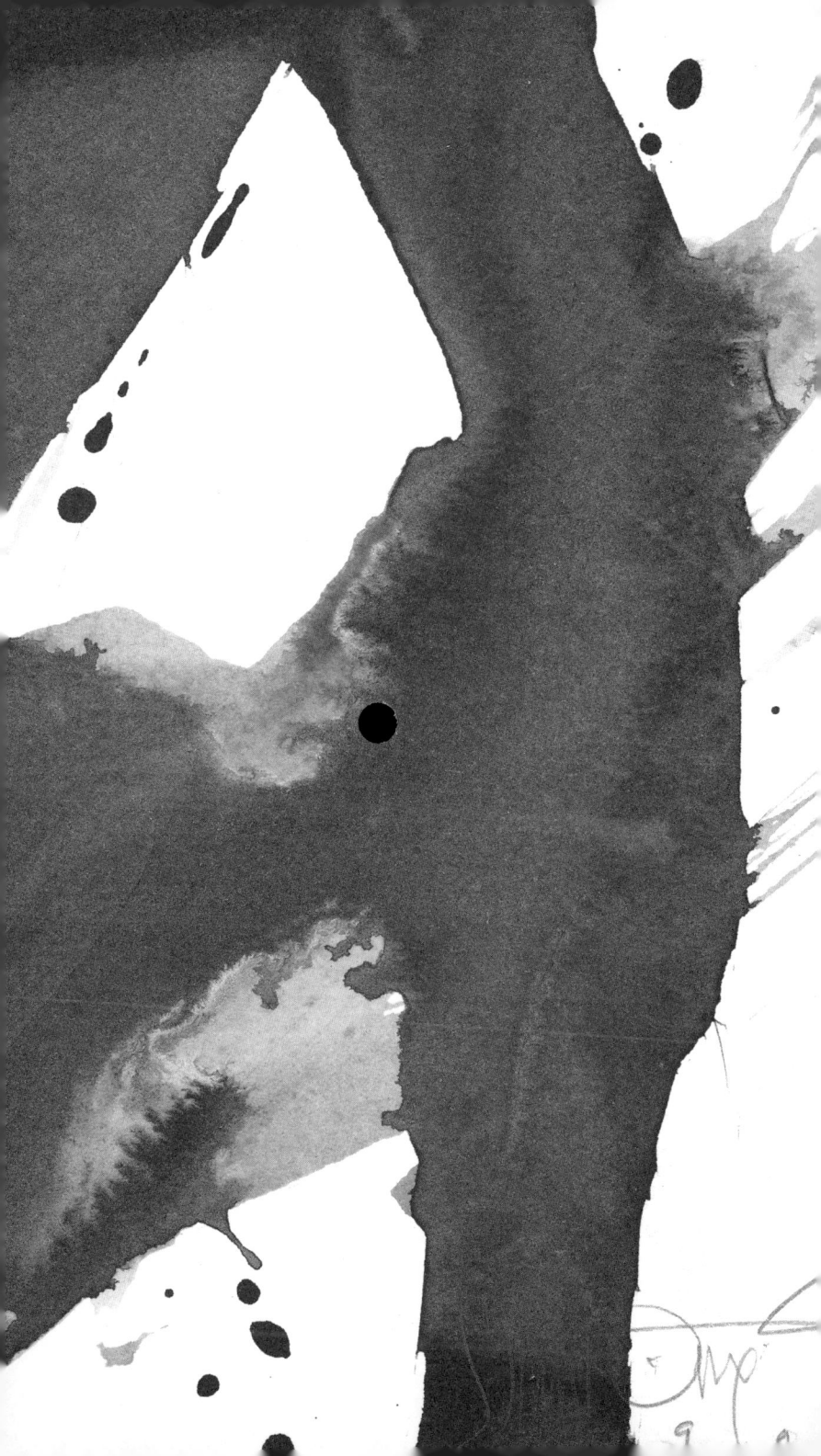

Matanović Manda, YUGOSLAVIA

(91)
gently alighting
a flock of crows
and snowflakes

Matas Duško, CROATIA

(92)
starry sky—
track with the moonlight
drifting with the boat

Matas Duško, CROATIA

●

raspberry picking—
the children's lips
grow red

McMaster Višnja, CROATIA

●

(94)
we pick chestnuts
in silence—the earth trembles
from the bombing

Mehle Jernej, SLOVENIA

(95)
riot squad—
gypsy woman draws deep
on her cigarette

Mijajlović - Adski Dušan, YUGOSLAVIA

●

(96)
falling snow—
people pass by carrying
nobody's flakes

Mijajlović - Adski Dušan, YUGOSLAVIA

(97)
between swaths
the mover brings a clover
in his hair

Mijatović Danilo, YUGOSLAVIA

(98)
midnight thunder—
the new year splits away
from the old

Mijović Tomislav, YUGOSLAVIA

(99)
city dump—
the northwind is whistling
in a bottleneck

Mijović Tomislav, YUGOSLAVIA

(100)
silence—
the sculptor and his head of clay
watching each other

Milenković Nebojša, YUGOSLAVIA

(101)
an old bus—
through the broken roof
summer clouds

Milenković Nebojša, YUGOSLAVIA

(102)
to the coal-seller
a beauty offering:
a little mirror

Milenković Vojislav, YUGOSLAVIA

(103)
January snow—
all the borders mixed
in our village

Mladenović Svetlana, YUGOSLAVIA

●

(104)
exposed cliff—
the lone pine holds
a cloud

Nešić Marija, YUGOSLAVIA

(105)
extinguished fire—
amidst the coals
a firefly

Nilić Nikola, YUGOSLAVIA

●

(106)
moonlight
river divides the forest
into two nights

Nilić Nikola, YUGOSLAVIA

(107)
in clusters
of white lilac
a raven even darker

Noyes H.F., GREECE

(108)
raking aside leaves
on the backyard pond
I release the moon

Noyes H.F., GREECE

●

(109)
cliffside siesta—
flow of the rock face
into my sleep

Noyes H.F., GREECE

(110)
a mist of stars—
mountain water flickering
through dark corn

Objedović Milivoj, CROATIA

scent of the lime tree—
on this sleepless evening
everyone is my neighbor

Ognjenović Mirjana, YUGOSLAVIA

(112)
snowy house—
the silence broken by
a sip of lime tea

Ognjenović Mirjana, YUGOSLAVIA

(113)
the sea at noon—
air filled with the smell
of fish and oleanders

Patrichi Radu, ROMANIA

●

(114)
autumn rain—
beneath a leaf, the nibbling
of a mouse

Pavić Aleksandar, YUGOSLAVIA

●

(115)　　going nowhere
during the air-raid alarm—
a scarecrow

Pavić Ivan, YUGOSLAVIA

(116)
in the grass
laid down by the wind
head of an old doll

Pečnik Franc, SLOVENIA

(117)
a man
in the grass drinks—
autumn sky

Pešić Predrag - Šera, YUGOSLAVIA

(118)
behind raspberry canes
i become a hidden ear
to one nightingale

Petreski Hristo, MACEDONIA

(119)
sour plum—
my mouth puckers
as she takes a bite

Petrović Zvonko, CROATIA

snowflakes fall
into the scent
of warm bread

Plažanin Darko, CROATIA

(121)
storm over—
a boy wipes the sky
from the table

Prodanović Živko, CROATIA

tomcat yawning on the terrace—
summer storm has gone by

Prokopiev Aleksandar, MACEDONIA

●

(123)
full moon—
shadow of my mother vanishes
behind the wall

Pšak Katarina, CROATIA

(124)
twinkling
through apricot blossoms
one thread of sun

Pšak Katarina, CROATIA

(125)
first bloom
of primrose—
its yellow smell

Raonić Zoran, YUGOSLAVIA

(126)
autumn sky—
a raven follows
fighting aircraft

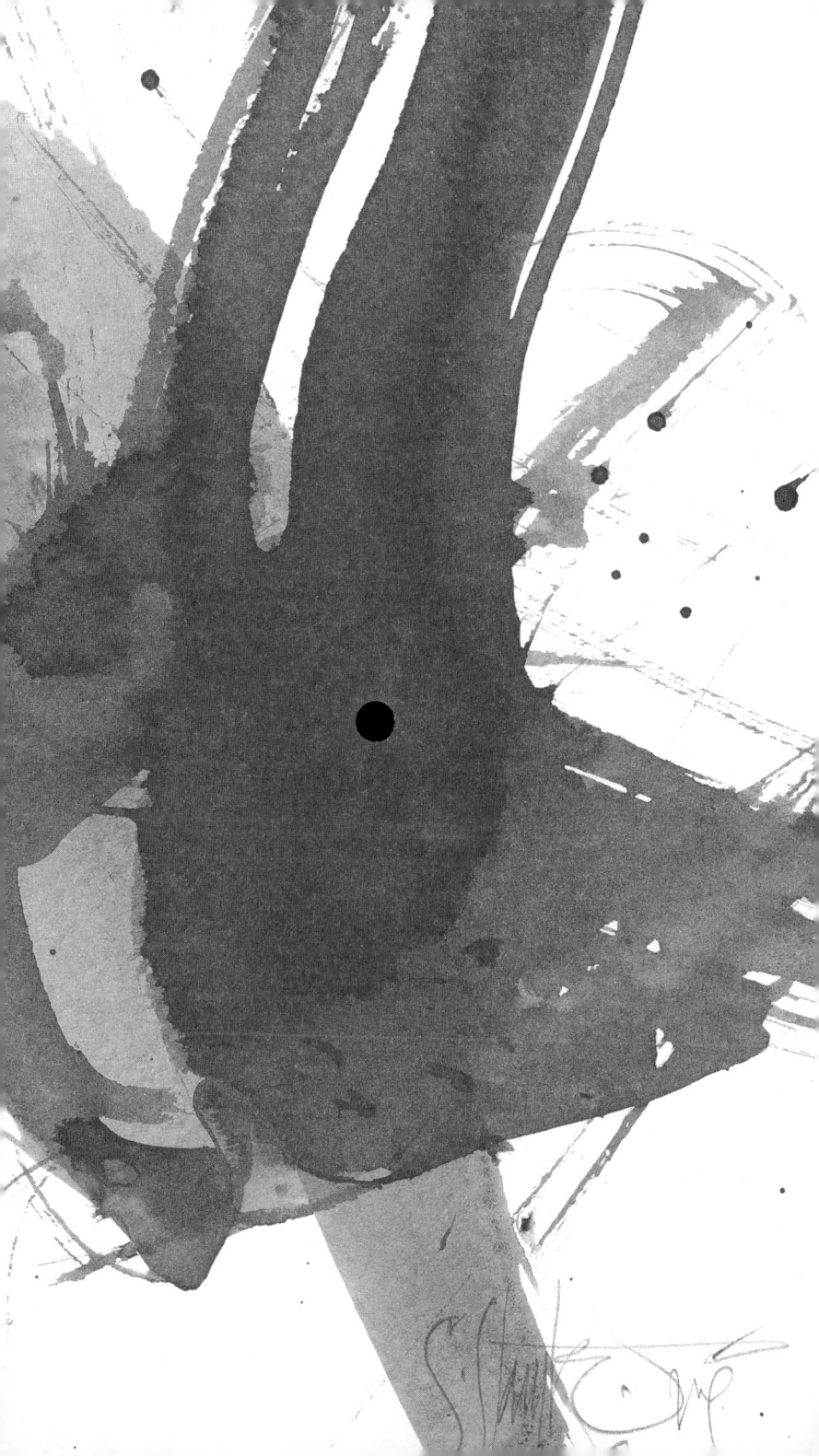

Rijavec Maja, CROATIA

(127)
frontier crossing:
aimlessly flying over,
white poplar seed

Ristić J. Dragan, YUGOSLAVIA

(128)
on the old log
a cat rubs itself lazy—
mild spring sun

Ristić J. Dragan, YUGOSLAVIA

(129)
bouquet of lilies—
in the cellophane wrapping
a wandering bee

Ristić J. Dragan, YUGOSLAVIA

(130)
lights out
before the air raid—
bright moon

Ruse Ana, ROMANIA

a ship moves
beyond the vanishing point—
the child's unfinished drawing

Sandu Liviu, ROMANIA

(132)
thunder—
the sentence remains unfinished
on the blackboard

Ševo Aleksandar, YUGOSLAVIA

(133)
autumn—
on the blackened fence
a wet sparrow

Šiački Olivera, YUGOSLAVIA

(134)
still life—
on the working table
the dust

Šiljak Mićun, YUGOSLAVIA

●

(135)   Igalo hotspring—
thinking about bombers
during a massage

Simin Nebojša, YUGOSLAVIA

●

(136) after the bombing
ruins of a bridge
linked by the fog

Smărăndescu Vasile, ROMANIA

●

(137)
sunset—
the corktree shade stretches
into the courtyared

Sotirova Raina, BULGARIA

(138)
stopped
along the pathway—
dog-rose in bloom

Španović Marinko, CROATIA

(139)

spring rain—
the lid is hopping
over boiling beans

Stamenković Mile, CROATIA

(140)
deserted town—
hungry war victims
feed the pigeons

Stanković Slavoljub, YUGOSLAVIA

●

(141) silence—
rustling of steps in the snow
and two shadows

Štebih Mihael, CROATIA

●

(142) flying between sky
and clouds
the tea is getting cold

Stefanov Dimitar, BULGARIA

●

(143)
the cold wind's roar—
unmistakeably a dog,
this knot in the beam

Stefanov Dimitar, BULGARIA

(144)
cold moon—
shadows within shadows
along the snowy road

Stefanov Dimitar, BULGARIA

●

(145)
boiling jam...
the night thickens
with sizzling

Stojanovski Bogdanka, YUGOSLAVIA

(146)
a pale shadow:
dragonfly has landed
on a leaf

Stojanovski Bogdanka, YUGOSLAVIA

●

(147)
the boats
prop up the sky
with the masts

Stojanović Živorad, YUGOSLAVIA

●

(148)   after plowing—
ants look for a new path
to the anthill

Stojičić Djoko, YUGOSLAVIA

●

(149)
rain stops—
clear and muddy streams
join together

Suciu Lucian, ROMANIA

(150)

gazing so long
at the clock—something inside me
comes to a stop

Theodoru Gh. Ştefan, ROMANIA

●

(151)   sparrow on the wing
with one more straw from the vest
of the old scarecrow

Tošić Ljubinka, YUGOSLAVIA

(152)
sharing the fields
of quarreling neighbors—
blooming blackberry

Tošić Ljubinka, YUGOSLAVIA

(153)
air-raid alarm—
the traffic light changes
for no one

Vasiliu Florin, ROMANIA

(154)

a boy in tears—
melted in his palm
all the snowflakes he gathered

Važić Saša, YUGOSLAVIA

(155)
bakery window—
the beggar before it white
with snow

Vitanov Gencho, BULGARIA

(156)

neon sign shining
on a porcelain tooth—
winter evening

Vučković Radoslav, YUGOSLAVIA

(157)
april rain
a rainbow joins
the two worlds

Vujić - Tomljanović Ljiljana, B & H

a screech-owl
and blacksmith's hammer
outcry each other

Vukasović Vid, YUGOSLAVIA

(159)
abandoned home—
huge snowflakes fall
down the chimney flue

Vukasović Vid, YUGOSLAVIA

(160)
autumn morning—
a shadow of a cloud
on the shadow of my hand

Vukasović Vid, YUGOSLAVIA

●

(161)
flock of wild geese
migrating this winter night
through my restless dreams

Zarnestri Ene Dumitru, ROMANIA

(162)
barracks—
at the recruit's window
hay scent

Živanović Radovan, YUGOSLAVIA

●

(163)
unexploded
yellow NATO bomb—
a field of dandelions

Zlatić - Kavgić Nada, YUGOSLAVIA

(164)
lingering summer—
putting a dried flower
in the herbarium

Zoe Savina, GREECE

(165)
evening—
the frog hops
with raindrops

Žegarac - Peharnik Milan, CROATIA

sunday quiet—
mountaineering songs
from the passing bus

Alain Kervern

TOWARDS A NEW PERCEPTION OF REALITY

To raise fundamental questions about place, role and power of Man in the Universe: this is to the western mind to perceive reality as a dialectical opposition between subjectivity and objectivity. The world affirms itself in this view according to two different realities: consciousness on one hand and things outside reach of thought on the other. In this system thought exists in autonomy and things form the entity that exists outside thought. Traditionally, subject enters through its spirit in contact with the outer Universe, because it understands and reconstructs the Universe through consideration and language. Employing senses this same subject perceives the existence of things in connection with its capacities. This way of perceiving reality determines a hermetic line of division between what is internal and external to itself. In this thought, only the interiority creates certainty - we think about the famous "I think, therefore I am" *cogito ergo sum* of Rene Descartes - and things are pushed to the outer world, unreal and delusive.

The concept of a strict demarcation line between two different spheres finds the most evident practical application in the field of painting. A very prosaic idea about line in the art of graphics functions as "a positive attribute and propriety of the object itself," says as philosopher Merleau-Ponty. "A line, that is contour of an apple," he explains, "or a border between the cultivated field and the prairie, which we accept as the reality of the word, where a pencil and a paintbrush only pass by."

But Leonardo da Vinci already expressed his doubts in this concept of a line. In his *Discussion about Painting* he invites "to discover in every object a special way in which a certain curved line moves over the whole of the area. This line is just like its generic axis." It is more an outlet of the energy than a demarcation line. Maybe it is none of the lines which could be seen in reality. In fact there is no line which could be seen itself alone." Neither a contour of an apple, nor a border between a field and a prairie are here and there... These lines should limit apple or prairie, but apple and prairie "create" by itself and appear in the world of visible as if they arrived from a "pre-univerzal world," answers Merleau-Ponty some centuries later.

That is how a new way of perceiving this reality develops in contrast with a very schematic vision of perception - radiation of the visible, life proper to things, which a painter looks for under the name of depth, place, colour, and a poet in the dynamics of sounds, rhythms of sentences, music of words. The way of seeing the world, which surpasses the preceding one, is inspired in the West by Husserl, Jean Paul Sartre, Merleau-Ponty. Subject is no more in a simple opposition to the world of objects, it is rather connected to these objects and to the world. Object, as appears to the consciousness, depends to the things and to subject, which percieves at the same time. To perceive, one should not be passive, since perceiving is not a state. One should look to see and listen to hear, because perception is action. Consciousness, discovery of the outer world, appear in connection with the others, is an interactive phenomenon, during which a subject constructs a structured and intelligible representation of the Universe of things. And the world is a result of a sensible construction of everyone's experience. The point is not in affirming certainties, based on the autonomous thought, which is concentrated in itself in the way Descartes did it; but in naming the world regarding the ties among individuals and things. The world exists as a phenomenon, perceived by the individuals in a certain culture, nourished by a personal story. Imagination of the individual does not oppose to the objective and independent world. The point is in exploring harmonies and encounters — awoken, multiplied and celebrated, between man and the world, which he perceives and constructs at the same time. It's this audacious and inventive dynamics which made Master Eckart say "God exists because the world exists".

A contemporary painter Oliver Debre finds himself in this phenomenon of interaction between the sensibility of the artist and reality: "When I'm like wind, like rain, like water which flows, I participate in nature and nature passes through me (...). I translate the emotion which is in me in front of nature, but not nature itself (...).
I wished we rejoiced the landscape as a new form of thought and not a natural landscape." Speaking about the same author, Toshio Yamanashi, a conservator at Kamakura Museum explains that "vast space, which exists outside cadre originally, seems attracted by it and to provoke communication between internal and external space we have to cause the awareness of the borders." This new concept of reality and this relation towards the World seem to approach the eastern vision where everything exists in a subtle game of interdependence. If the painter Monet touched the hearts of the Japanese, it happened mostly because "tracing the light playing on the nenuphars in his garden, he somehow surpassed the

impressionism," notes painter Yasse Tabuchi, who continues: "There was light and nothing escaped from it. Every being was nothing else but a game of interferences with light. And that made the nenuphars of our visionary painter float."

A perfect connoisseur of eastern and western sensibilities, painter Tabuchi asks himself about two conceptions of the world: "Emptiness, voidness, nought: This is zone of a moving sable. The western representation of the world is here in opposition to the eastern one. Let's take a symbol of a circle, for example. Is nought inside the circle? Or is it outside? Is emptines inside or outside? For the west this abyss is a terrifiying place of nonexistence." And western philosophers mobilized their energy to limit the consequences of this vertigo.

The taoistic thought on the contrary inverses the logic of the symbolism. According to this thought all of the "10 000 beings" of the Universe are within this mystic circle. The Tao way, the energy of the emptiness, born out of primordial voidness "circles around these '10 000 beings' and prescribes them with the creative flux. In this case circle does not indicate the border between 'having' and 'non having' . The circle in this cosmical sphere is only a membrane, where 'having' and 'non — having' mingle mysteriously" explains Yasse Tabuchi. So, we can say now that our senses intercept "messages from the outside through rumors, which they rouse in us" as Merleau-Ponty formulated in his essay *The eye and spirit*.

The frontier between interior and exterior is no more an obstacle, but a place of transition and exchange, a fertile tie between two realities. A painter interrogates light, reflection, shadow, how they arise suddenly, to teach us to see, while a poet celebrates only a miracle always, this continuous transition between visible and invisible. A poet writes from dictation of his inner thought and word, while a painter reveals that things are looking at him. The artistic expression becomes an adventure in which "thought doesn't want to frighten the visible, but decides to create it according to a chosen pattern instead," says Merleau-Ponty. Artistic expression leads to a deposit of solidarity between a reader and a poet, a painter and an observer, a listener and a musician. There's no need anymore to speak about place, sound, light,... We should rather encourage, light to start talking, or sounds to resonate. The artist is born when the perceptible concentrates and become aware of itself. Apollinaire said that poems are sentences which seems not to be created — they were made by themselves.

Can we compare this new concept of perception with a considerable development of short poetry inspired by Japanese haiku around the world ? There's no doubt that research of new expression modes corresponds to a new manner of conceiving reality, to a true phenomenologic revolution. Recent evolution of poetical dynamic inspired by haiku could be one of the manifestations of this research.

In a recent essay, issued in a Japanese poetry magazine Ginyu (The Narrator), the critic and poet Toru Sudo reminds us of Masaoka Shiki (1867 - 1902), who played an important role when haiku adapted to a sensibility of its epoch. Shiki noted two types of progressions in the art of composing poems: one connected with beginners who gradually achieve a satisfactory degree of mastery; and one of accomplished poets, who experience realms, never before experienced by their forerunners. The second ones gained the attention of Shiki, for whom Hekogoto Kawahigashi (1873 - 1937) was a true representative of these audacious and fertile explorers. In Japan from the beginning of this century the social and economic changes were rapid and irreversible. Shiki observed that a literary and artistic expression went through the metamorphoses caused by the evolution of a public taste due to a progress of the obligatory instructions. The same was true for haiku. It changed many times during these years. Despite the convenience of this analysis, haiku has been driven far away from its neoclassical way of the beginning of the century. From this time on esthetical preoccupation of haiku remains the art of singing about " roses, birds, wind and moon ", and the development of a " sketch concept painted after nature " (Shasei) which Shiki stated to be a creative principle. The 5-7-5 syllables metrics, obligatory introduction with the season word and the presence of cutting words are still essential rules.

After the success of the beginning of the century, haiku has become boring and faint today. The "impressionistic" style, which haiku challenged, lost its inspiration. To look at the Universe from another angle, we need new tools. The Japanese haiku of the coming century must regenerate (Toru Sudo) and surpass conventional esthetic. To liberate haiku so that it would adapt and correspond with new sensibilities means to give up all that makes it purely visual, inconsistent, superficial.

With the internationalization of haiku we witness undoubtedly the birth of a new type of poetry — haiku of planetary dimension, gathering from the human depth, rich in references which belong to all the members of the same community and reveal a human and universal archetype while at the same time representing the world. Every haiku becomes a condensation of energy, which breaks the conventions and supports new organization of the world.

The non-Japanese contribute to the renovation of haiku and often their innovations break the sacred rules of haiku, whose traditional sources of inspiration become extinct. All around the world the gifted haiku writers have learned to catch in some few words, on the surface of reality, the trembling of the depth.

The present anthology is without doubt an important step on the way towards a new, different haiku. Its contributions to the renovation of this form lies in the originality of its sources of inspiration, strong personalities of both women and men who express the parts of themselves in this book, in their sharp talent provoking a slight loss of balance which shakes every certainty, every indifference, every conformity.

●

ABOUT THE EDITORS

●

DIMITAR ANAKIEV, is a poet, editor and publisher. He owns Prijatelj Haiku Press which publishes books and magazines of and about haiku, including *Knots* and *Piece of Sky*. He is the "father" and editor of many haiku projects in Southeastern Europe such as: *Haiku Novine* in Niš, Yugoslavia, and *Prijatelj* in Tolmin, Slovenia. He has eleven haiku books published. His books include *Ptičija Staza* (Prosveta, Niš, 1995) in Serbian, Ptica Pateka (Matom, Sofia, 1996) in Bulgarian, Lastovke (Apokalipsa, Ljubljana, 1998) in Slovenian, and *Enormous Frog* (Prijatelj, Tolmin, 1998) in English. He also has won several prizes in haiku competitions such as Second Prize in *The Mainichi Daily News* Contest in 1993. Actualy he chairs the inaugural committee of the Haiku Association of South East Europe (HASEE) and edits Green Apples - Forum for International Haiku.

JIM KACIAN is a writer, publisher and tennis professional who lives near the Shenandoah River in Virginia. He is the author of five books (*Presents of Mind*, 1995; *Chincoteague*, 1996; *Six Directions*, 1997; *In Concert*, 1998; and forthcoming *Out of the Stones: Selected Haiku of Jim Kacian*). He owns Red Moon Press, the largest and most prestigious publisher of English-language haiku in the world, and is editor-in-chief for the *Red Moon Haiku Anthology* series. He also edits *Frogpond*, the international magazine of the Haiku Society of America.

AUTHOR INDEX

Abălută, Konstantin 1
Adjanski, Pavle 2
Alexe, Gabriele 3
Anakiev, Alma 4
Anakiev, Dimitar 5, 6, 7

Bambić, Maša 8
Bebek, Robert 9, 10, 11
Banea, Ştefan 12
Bilankov, Smiljka 13
Bizjak, Zvonka 14
Boban, Nediljko 15, 16
Božin, Mirjana 17
Bratić, Ilija 18
Brcanović, Valentina 19
Brnović, Veselin 20
Bubanja, Vojislav 21
Bukva, Borivoj 22
Busioc, E. Valentin 23, 24, 25
Bušić, Franko 26

Čekolj, Marijan 27, 28, 29
Čevanić, Majska 30
Ćirović - Ljutički, Milenko 31
Codrescu, Ion 32, 33, 34
Čopa, Miroslav 35, 36

Ciubotariu, Manta Elena 37
Crnomarković, Ileana 38
Cvetanović, Vidoje 39
Cvetković, Predrag 40, 41

Dacić, Rade 42
Dejanović, Goran 43
Denjo, Mirsad 44
Devidé, Vladimir 45, 46, 47
Dimić, Moma 48
Djurbabić, Svetomir 49
Djuričić, Ljiljana 50
Djurišić, Dušan 51, 52
Doderović, Zoran 53, 54, 55
Doman, Dan 56, 57
Dumitresku, Emilia 58
Dumitru, Radu 59
Duțu, Olga 60

Faraon, Eugenia 61
Funda, Željko 62

Gagić, Smiljka 63
Gašpar, Dragica 64
Gečić, Anica 65

Hamazin, Ana 66
Hohnjec, Josip 67
Hudnik, Marko 68

Iacob, P. Ion 69
Ifrim, Clilea 70
Ilijevska - Jovanovska, Pandora 71
Ioannou, Costas 72
Isaic, Cătălin 73
Ivančan, Dubravko 74, 75, 76

Jegdić, Branka 77
Jembrih, Ivica 78
Joksimović, Zorica 79
Jovanović, Bojan 80

Kalač, Hamdija 81
Kovačević, Ivan 82, 83
Krizmanić, Franjo 84

Mančić, Olga - Lodika   85
Manić - Forski, Dragoslav 86
Maretić, Tomislav 87, 88, 89
Marijanović, Dubravko 90
Matanović, Manda 91
Matas, Duško 92, 93
McMaster, Višnja 94
Mehle, Jernej 95
Mijajlović - Adski, Dušan 96, 97
Mijatović, Danilo 98
Mijović, Tomislav 99, 100
Milenković, Nebojša 101, 102
Milenković, Vojislav 103
Mladenović, Svetlana 104

Nešić, Marija 105
Nilić, Nikola 106, 107
Noyes, H.F. 108, 109, 110

Objedović, Milivoj 111
Ognjenović, Mirjana 112, 113

Patrichi, Radu 114
Pavić, Aleksandar 115
Pavić, Ivan 116
Pečnik, Franc 117
Pešić, Predrag - Šera 118
Petreski, Hristo 119
Petrović, Zvonko 120
Plažanin, Darko 121
Prodanović, Živko 122
Prokopiev, Aleksandar 123
Pšak, Katarina 124, 125

Raonić, Zoran 126
Rijavec, Maja 127
Ristić J. Dragan 128, 129, 130
Ruse, Ana 131

Sandu, Liviu 132
Ševo, Aleksandar 133
Šiački, Olivera 134
Šiljak, Mićun 135
Simin, Nebojša 136
Smărăndescu, Vasile 137

Sotirova, Raina 138
Španović, Marinko 139
Stamenković, Mile 140
Stanković, Slavoljub 141
Štebih, Mihael 142
Stefanov, Dimitar 143, 144, 145
Stojanovski, Bogdanka 146, 147
Stojanović, Živorad 148
Stojičić, Djoko 149
Suciu, Lucian 150

Theodoru, Gh. Ştefan   151
Tošić, Ljubinka 152,   153

Vasiliu, Florin 154
Važić, Saša 155
Vitanov, Gencho 156
Vučković, Radoslav 157
Vujić - Tomljanović, Ljiljana 158
Vukasović, Vid 159, 160, 161

Zarnestri, Ene Dumitru 162
Živanović, Radovan 163
Zlatić - Kavgić, Nada 164
Zoe, Savina 165
Žegarac - Peharnik, Milan 166

CONTENTS

FROM MOVEMENT TO LITERATURE,
Dimitar Anakiev 7
TAPPING THE COMMON WELL, Jim Kacian . . 15

Konstantin Abălută 23
Pavle Adjanski 24
Gabriele Alex 25
Alma Anakiev 26
Dimitar Anakiev 27
Maša Bambić 30
Robert Bebek 31
Ştefan Banea 34
Smiljka Bilankov 35
Zvonka Bizjak 36
Nediljko Boban 37
Mirjana Božin 39
Ilija Bratić 40
Valentina Brcanović 43
Veselin Brnović 44
Vojislav Bubanja 45
Borivoj Bukva 46
Valentin E. Busioc 47
Franko Bušić 50
Marijan Čekolj 51
Majska Čevanić 54
Milenko Ćirović - Ljutički 55
Ion Codrescu 56

Miroslav Čopa	59
Elena Manta Ciubotariu	63
Ileana Crnomarković	64
Vidoje Cvetanović	65
Predrag Cvetković	66
Rade Dacić	68
Goran Dejanović	69
Mirsad Denjo	70
Vladimir Devidé	71
Moma Dimić	74
Svetomir Djurbabić	75
Ljiljana Djuričić	76
Dušan Djurišić	77
Zoran Doderović	79
Dan Doman	84
Emilia Dumitresku	86
Radu Dumitru	87
Olga Duţu	88
Eugenia Faraon	89
Željko Funda	90
Smiljka Gagić	91
Dragica Gašpar	92
Anica Gečić	93
Ana Hamazin	94
Josip Hohnjec	95
Marko Hudnik	96
Ion P. Iacob	97
Clilea Ifrim	98
Pandora Ilijevska - Jovanovska	99

Costas Ioannou	100
Cătălin Isaic	103
Dubravko Ivančan	104
Branka Jegdić	107
Ivica Jembrih	108
Zorica Joksimović	109
Bojan Jovanović	110
Hamdija Kalač	111
Ivan Kovačević	112
Franjo Krizmanić	114
Olga Mančić - Lodika	115
Dragoslav Manić - Forski	116
Tomislav Maretić	117
Dubravko Marijanović	120
Manda Matanović	123
Duško Matas	124
Višnja McMaster	126
Jernej Mehle	127
Dušan Mijajlović - Adski	128
Danilo Mijatović	130
Tomislav Mijović	131
Nebojša Milenković	133
Vojislav Milenković	135
Svetlana Mladenović	136
Marija Nešić	137
Nikola Nilić	138
H.F. Noyes	140
Milivoj Objedović	145
Mirjana Ognjenović	146

Radu Patrichi	148
Aleksandar Pavić	149
Ivan Pavić	150
Franc Pečnik	151
Predrag Pešić - Šera	152
Hristo Petreski	153
Zvonko Petrović	154
Darko Plažanin	155
Živko Prodanović	156
Aleksandar Prokopiev	157
Katarina Pšak	158
Zoran Raonić	160
Maja Rijavec	163
Dragan J. Ristić	164
Ana Ruse	167
Liviu Sandu	168
Aleksandar Ševo	169
Olivera Šiački	170
Mićun Šiljak	171
Nebojša Simin	172
Vasile Smărăndescu	173
Raina Sotirova	174
Marinko Španović	175
Mile Stamenković	176
Slavoljub Stanković	177
Mihael Štebih	178
Dimitar Stefanov	179
Bogdanka Stojanovski	184
Živorad Stojanović	186

Djoko Stojičić 187
Lucian Suciu 188
Ştefan Gh. Theodoru 189
Ljubinka Tošić 190
Florin Vasiliu 192
Saša Važić 193
Gencho Vitanov 194
Radoslav Vučković 195
Ljiljana Vujić - Tomljanović 196
Vid Vukasović 197
Dumitru Ene Zarnestri 200
Radovan Živanović 203
Nada Zlatić - Kavgić 204
Savina Zoe 205
Milan Žegarac - Peharnik 206

TOWARDS A NEW PERCEPTION OF REALITY,
Alain Kervern 209
ABOUT THE EDITORS 219
AUTHOR INDEX 223

THE ANTHOLOGY OF SOUTHEASTERN EUROPEAN HAIKU POETRY

●

Editors: Dimitar Anakiev & Jim Kacian
Design & Illustrations: Slavoljub Stanković
Typography: ITC Veljovic by Jovica Veljović
Print: Grafika Art, Tolmin, Slovenia

Publisher: Prijatelj Haiku Press,
          Brunov drevored 19
          5220 Tolmin
          Slovenia

Distributors: Red Moon Press, P.O.Box 2461,
             Winchester, VA, 22604-1661 USA;
             Prijatelj, Brunov drevored 19, 5220
             Tolmin, Slovenia, EU

ISBN 961-90715-0-8
Copyright ©1999 by Dimitar Anakiev & Jim Kacian
Illustrations © 1999 by Slavoljub Stanković
All right reserved.